STATUS OF THE MOURNED

Also by Hugh Seidman

Collecting Evidence (1970)
Blood Lord (1974)
Throne / Falcon / Eye (1982)
People Live, They Have Lives (1992)
Selected Poems: 1965-1995 (1995)
Somebody Stand Up and Sing (2005)

STATUS OF THE MOURNED

HUGH SEIDMAN

DISPATCHES  EDITIONS

The author thanks the following print and/or web venues for publishing some version of the indicated poems. Also, where applicable, versions are listed in ascending order, from earliest to latest. An asterisk (*) flags the same version of a poem in two different venues at different times.

"1928," *House Organ;* "Abingdon Square Park," *The Ocean State Review;* "A Great Wind Is Bearing Me Across the Sky," T*he Laurel Review;* "Art," *Fowl Feathered Review* (http://fowlpoxpress. ca/); "Conquest of Peru," 1. *Columbia Review,* 2. *Big Bridge* (www.bigbridge.org), 3. *Resist Much / Obey Little;* "Crossing Bryant Park," 1. *The Cafe Review,* 2. *High Chair* (www.highchair. com.ph); "Einstein on the Beach," *Granta* (www.granta.com); "For Jayne," *The Laurel Review;* "Frank Canned, Joe Upped" (*), 1. *Live Mag,* 2. *Dispatches from the Poetry Wars* (http:// dispatchespoetrywars.com); "Lava," *Provincetown Arts;* "Like Anyone," *The Cincinnati Review;* "L.Z." (*), 1. *House Organ,* 2. *Dispatches from the Poetry Wars* (http://dispatchespoetrywars.com); "Many Have Written this Poem," *Dispatches from the Poetry Wars* (http://dispatchespoetrywars. com); "Marla Ruzicka," *Big Bridge* (www.bigbridge.org); "Millennial," *Dispatches from the Poetry Wars* (http://dispatchespoetrywars.com); "New Year," *Big City Lit* (www.bigcitylit.com); "Poems," 1. *A Festschrift for Clayton Eshleman,* 2. *Columbia Review,* 3. *Big City Lit* (www.bigcitylit.com); "Seido Karate: 'Kino Hito No Mi Kyo No Wagami,'" *The Saint Ann's Review;* "Statements for Poetry," *Dispatches from the Poetry Wars* (http://dispatchespoetrywars.com); "The Longing of the New World for the Old World," *The Ocean State Review;* "The Train Explodes," *The Cincinnati Review;* "Unfinished Poem," 1. *The Cafe Review,* 2. *High Chair* (www.highchair.com.ph); "Vienna," *The Saint Ann's Review;* "'Writing and Catastrophe,'" 1. *Fowl Feathered Review* (http:// fowlpoxpress.ca/), 2. *Resist Much / Obey Little;* "Without Irony," *Resist Much / Obey Little;* "Zuk Poem," *FlashPoint* (www.flashpointmag.com).

Cover painting:
Converging Road I (detail) by Jayne Holsinger, 1998.
Oil on wood panel.
12 x 12 inches.
(www.jayneholsinger.com)

LCCN Cataloging information applied for.
ISBN 978-1-947980-99-0

Dispatches Editions is an imprint of Spuyten Duyvil Press
Write to: poetrywardispatch@gmail.com

CONTENTS

For Jayne Holsinger

OLD LETTER

Passion of the written when all whom I knew were alive
Helping you will not in any way burden us in any way whatsoever

Like the theory of the future of the visible stars
So far-flung in the blank sky that their light will not reach us

You being happy makes us doubly happy
You are our life and joy—no matter what the psychology books say

And my father in motion fated like the voided stars
One who has gone light years by now—who would help if he could

LAVA

Six-month, street-ditched tot.
Psycho Mom walks off.

ECT tit swapped for Dad.
Talk about mixed metaphor!

Shocked Mom comes home.
Babe's bed at parents' bulb.

Past it, Freudian strobe.
Had that shut sonny up?

Did not talk until three.
Doc said: a spew, if ready.

Yes—fire-smart, avid.
Cooled to paradox of rock.

Yet Mom spat: rotten brat.
E.g., babe nixes galoshes.

But—why not rebirth?
Not the re-screwed watts.

Stubborn rubbers jabber?
Either way, whacked Pompeii.

THE GREAT VEHICLE

M66 to Dr. Z.
Sometimes, maid's
butter cookies, tea.

Prone, sullen; until,
not per Sigmund:
sat up, faced front.

Rep tie, vested suit,
cordovan shoes:
rehearsing the adult.

Premier soon. But
first, ardor—nuts
affaire de coeur.

Paramour glowing.
Bored with boy-
friend? God knows.

Finally, Dr. Z, ill,
dozing in sessions.
Dad, once, palpable.

Thanksgiving eve:
The *Court Jester.*
Wind shook leaves.

A Montecristo 4
soothed dreams.
Decades fell/rose.

Psyched spring,
new tears, long ago.
Perhaps tomorrow.

Subway ad lasers
tattoo, scar, mole:
Dr. Z's son "Dr. Z."

Bestir the zombie?
Hot rerun: *Night
of the Live Dead.*

Frank Canned, Joe Upped

Something awry in the methane storms on Jupiter.
Something misfiring in the enzyme switches of memory.

Rage: a steel bar to bite.

But then, as always there is *but then*, past Liberty, past Hudson, past harbor.
A vanishing bird skein in the watered-out October orange.

The sudden, tectonic rupture of language, starting migration.

To console Frank, perhaps, or even Joe.
Fucked Frank, genius Joe.

INFARCT

1 BEGINNER'S BRAIN

Post attack, cut self slack?
Henry Irving stroked.

Niedecker down that year.
Rumi, too, a year before.

LAD stent; Dad's IU fear.
Trudger, hopeless hoper.

Scar in lead "aVL"?
Cold star, love's failure.

Close closer, not wiser.
Urged to get back to life.

The living lives lived.
Mind kept off things.

Elsewhere, Henry's Hamlet.
Cri de coeur, for sure.

2 BLUE WHALE

Heart: clown-car large.
Aorta that can hold a child.

Elephant-heavy tongue.
Blow-spout breath of God.

Circler who starts.
Athwart the waters of God.

Lifespan of a child.
Fluke like the wing of a god.

Baleen behemoths' keen.
Leviathan sunk to God.

Circus car a child saw.
Honked clown horn.

Child crawls to chamber.
Blind bone worms gorge.

Envy

Once: Musketeer, soul chum, "brother."
Then: self-exalter, cocksure strutter.

No nameless Midas met minus a glance.
But galler, compeer, top dog, shunner.

I glared from that skewed level.
One foot in the present, one foot in the past.

Sane brain urged: let other prosper.
One wins today; one, tomorrow.

Instead: I signed the chit; I bought the myth.
200-dollar Brioni marked 29.

Silk treasure, paisley verdure.
Four-in-Hand, Pratt, Windsor, Half-Windsor.

Narcissus: unbudged, mirrored.
Knotted, noosed cravat at buttoned collar.

Between "Said" and "Is"

If I went somewhere; if I did something.
I'm so lucky.

Ambassador of good intentions.
The buildings will remember.

Day dream; see the sights.
Subjects fit for the odes.

Laud the local.
My "first-world" neighborhood.

Some would give right arms to be here.
Into the Mother's Day noon.

Mine in her plot.
22 years as I count.

I should sit with her as I have not.
Though soon enough to join her.

As someone soaps a face.
As someone circles the globe.

Earlobe's mirrored droplet of water.
As in the photo at 12.

Posed from a swim with Jay Pensak and Saul Posner.
Hung between "said" and "is."

Jewel as at any such ear that has ever been.
I would imagine.

MANY HAVE WRITTEN THIS POEM

Unveiled morning ceiling. You've
flown to see your mom in Illinois.

Blurted that you want fire, that
your bank book is in the flat file.

One weekend—Vermont headstones:
deer/lake; 18-wheeler; dog/angler.

Joked, we'd tenant, if hard luck,
Dad's Beth Moses plots in Pinelawn.

But now the desired urn—like your
dad's in dirt at your sister's farm.

I dreaded parental eternity, but
how lie with you—if ash—as flesh?

Two decoupled in the next world.
Recouped progeny at last breath.

MELANCHOLIA

On Ed's way out I bragged: I found the path.
Muzzled the black pit bull at 70-plus.

Tumors in the head of my boyhood friend Ed.
Three scalpeled, three gamma-knifed.

Metastatic melanoma—then, the grand mal.
Suddenly the ambulance woke me for a while.

Irony of Ed: Columbia imager of brains.
Claremont home hospice—a "life," as is claimed.

Ambition that enacts the acts of its plan.
To love, to work—for as long as one stands.

But underworlds smoldered and flared.
I could not forget what I could not remember.

The black pit bull again licked my hand.
Manic tongue of the clamped, adamant jaw.

TESTAMENT

I did not understand what no child meant since I had no child.
I did not understand a good death until my friend died and I had no friend.

Bereft words.
Powerless at the speed of Earth.

My wife—torn ankle—sleeps on the couch.
I wake in the loft in the blackness.

If she should die is no proxy left?
I must decide such facts with one who bills me hourly like a stranger.

My wife—torn ankle—hobbles on the earth.
She cannot climb the rungs to the bed.

Testate estate.
State shall not arbitrate.

I must redact my fate with the intimate exactness of the stranger.
Father mother brother sister child friend.

SEIDO KARATE

7 times down, 8 times up.
Shin sha—deeply appreciate.

Breath wets *Kagami Biraki* mirrors.
Handshakes heal the depressed.

Master: bare-hands sword catch.
100 men beaten, full contact.

Master: man like another.
Sphinx sitting *seiza* like none.

"I hit hard as I am your friend."
Bowing to orders of sweat.

Form not force, spirit not form.
Ichigeki hissatsu—blow kills ego.

Father's bicep, Mother's breast.
Art, martial art—no ax ground.

SEIDO KARATE: "KINO HITO NO MI KYO NO WAGAMI"[1]

—FOR ERNESTO RAIA (1937-2006)

butt on heels, right palm up in the lap under left knuckles, thumbs touching

I shut my eyes and shot a ray of invisible light to Beth Israel hospital
to the first female *sensei*—as the Master had instructed

tube-entwined, eyelids fluttering under the morphine—she had not known him
and then we stood when he struck the gong

and the tears arose that I would not have accorded myself
as if then for her with whom I had no connection

that night street shouts woke me from the plot of the only child
hunched with its head in its hands as if no one cared if it lived or died

the next day was Saturday and the sun racked my head
with its more-than-visible rays of light in the first definite day of summer

though she—alive below the noon—now breathed with the mourned
as I sipped my coffee in the park still starving in the tantrum of dream

and then I was down on the subway again to sit *seiza* before *kumite*
upon the track to no end but the speed of the hurtling body

amid the remarkable fervor that raises the dead to the status of the living

---

1 "Yesterday the Other Person, Today Myself"

GRAND MAL
—EDWARD E. SMITH (1940-2012)

salt water wracking metal
salt water rupturing buckled metal

a melanoma a frothing at the mouth
eyes rolled up into the head

the convulsed ocean the metastatic sky
conjoined to the tumoral brain

cremation ashes beside a bed
glacier melt thinned-out beaver pelt

sand foam churned by the salt
Pied Piper child shut in the wave

2

FOR JAYNE

Orphaned, punched, sold girl,
jumps to motorway cars in the film.

Homeless jogger in the yard,
at the shelter where you volunteer.

Up at five, shaves, to try for a job.

But no art need prove gravity;
no beard need test the razor.

I wanted *Webster's* all day,
to atone for ignorance of words.

To bar can't/cant from one *true* poem.
O banality!

Words that jar the coma of solitude.

You, teaching, clad in "hose,"
bone-chilled, catching cold in snow.

Hose, old word, Mother's word,
pubertal sexual echo of clothes.

Like *tears* for the martyr,
like *alms* for the supplicator.

Salves a moment—mauled, cut world.

FAME

river of the heart as is said as is written there is a little time
pewter sky an opened vein of the molten

body in black at the ATMs ashen hair spiked platinum
stared-at receipt momentary lowered armature of shoulders

not the immutable eyes of Penthesilea but Minerva's crow's-feet
piston fired on the high-octane post-modern

eroticized gravitons penetrating musculature
foot leg arm trunk satiating the voyeur

and then she was merely herself again forced forward toward vault
fate of matter noted here unashamedly still shrugged off

LOA

millions of tints and shades streaming in the rain
spectra of the mud aside from the temblors of an island

but the prismatic succumbed to the labyrinthal alleys
shut past the mainlands of love

and no path veered from the drum
from the throat-cut chicken goat bull

it was not possible to part the dark
hardened like the crust of a wound

where the green-eyed charnel blonde
unfurled the black-and-purple shroud

sweating and drunk on chilies and rum
knotting together some modest sister's corpse big toes at the road

cement breaker machete gangstress curses howler
bulldozer of the rigor-mortised bone statues

LOUSE POINT THONG

Who says you can't step into the same bay twice?

In the personals the would-be inflate.
Still, what fool mocks desire?

Lusty, loves-to-travel, blonde Ph.D.
30 years past Christ crucified.

Butt bare—as not in that day.
Not amiss, I guess, where the elegant osprey nests.

Same old, same old.
Sky, horizon, sun, cloud.

Remembering my ex-student's beachy, torrid kiss.
Horny swimsuit spurt.

Wading in cold.
No chill if the *qi* is up.

Who says you can't step into the same bay twice?

Last day at the *déjà vu* glitter.
Pixels infixed, later, in hard-drive New York.

L.R.

Forked sycamore gores the moon.
Piebald bark wrinkled like skin.

Notch between here and there.
Gash between now and then.

Hunger cites the giver of bread.
Gap-toothed, supermodel smile of that day.

Your embrace as if the world burned.
Gin and Dubonnet.

Brown sparrow, sooty pigeon doze.
Faux gas lamps incandesce paths.

Again you are the eidolon of mercy.
Again more than one can say.

Cold blown from cold.
White smoke torn from roofs.

Past as present: impervious, everywhere.
Trembling lips of ravenous gratitude.

ON SOME NIGHTS

On some nights my wife, who is my heart,
retreats to the TV as she had as a child.

Zones out at films seen before
or at shows having zero to do with her.

But if as a husband I balk, stupidly or wisely,
she nods and smiles, "I love you."

Or if I brood on a life or on an art,
she notes that I am doing "just fine."

As indeed I am in the summer wind,
divorced from whatever cry of the poem.

Even if just today I critiqued a book
for pay in books of or on this one or that one.

That which had null to do with whatever
once might have stood for a life or an art.

Juvenescent

—for M.L.

Cool August Friday after days of heat.

Purity of memory—
freed from the work week.

Is constraint what it takes?

Once, nonchalantly, on a couch, amid friends,
my hand wedged inside the back of your jeans.

Your stifled breath
I breathe to think on.

Clouds: slow, fast—like time itself.

Lost in the aureole.
Lost in the visceral rose.

But to have forced liberty,
to have exerted probe.

Years later, you appeared.

To make me make you make me uphold
why I had let you let me do what I had.

IRENE

Sebastian Tended by The Holy Women
—RIBERA, 1621

Wrist: upraised,
Strapped, affixed.

Sorrow arrows:
Armpit, hip—

Vectors toward her
Eye, his sex.

●

Triangle: his hand,
Hers; angel eye.

Angle bisectors
Stab saints' pupils,

Cross at third's
Left forefinger.

●

Inverted apex
Touches crux:

Her forceps fingers
Extort shaft.

Third eyes us:
Scorn moon.

•

Euclidean faith.
Exigent breath.

In four centuries:
Taut black dress.

T.G.I.F.
Still all business.

•

Strung sinew.
Martyr-hot bolt.

Pure compassion.
Anointed lesion.

CROSSING BRYANT PARK

—SUSAN ROBERTSON (1943-1997)

Rink down—up last fall mirroring summer.
1200 steps to work—Seventh to Madison.

First, past 50—your bridal two-step.
New, wet grass invoking *tomb*.

•

Father: suicide; Mother: survivor; Sister: fatal breast.
Tai chi fighter, shrink, scholarship Bryn Mawr waif.

Lungs sicker than said or known.
Phone small talk—then you were gone.

•

10,000 years ago: not statue, urn, stone.
10,000 years ago: sexual proof of lives.

Left you that August—who shall say why?
Hammocked dozer; oil-slick lake rainbow.

•

10,000 years ago: hope—oldest karma.
10,000 years ago: friends—*forever*.

Also—noduled, cut out womb.
Transfusion, perhaps, the future tumor root.

•

Tall, rawboned girl, in a brown poncho.
Memoir of the body—10,000 years ago.

Tears upon tears—more than for anyone.
Susan—do you yet smile at dull woe?

•

High-heeled graduates' pale lilies, arterial roses.
A couple's extravagant, tortuous kisses.

Heard your name, as if called.
Neurons that will not be annulled.

•

Nothing to do but abhor the wind.
Implored the immortals for solace.

Smut-mouthed Brigitte: vulva peppers, black rooster.
Red-tongued Kali: lei of heads, corpse trampler.

•

Reached at last—furnace blast.
A few pounds of dust, ash, bone.

Carbon tundra turning under suns.
Born to your planet—less than a grass pebble.

3

ABINGDON SQUARE PARK

Bronze doughboy's Colt pistol.
Spring's nursing-home invalids.

Are most good? Some mad?
Qin Shi Huang, first emperor.

Burned books, interred scholars.
Drank mercury for immortality.

Slaves moiled at his Great Wall.
Dug his *Lishan* mausoleum.

Kept by the terracotta goliaths.
When he croaked—civil war.

History etched as the long haul.
Though thugs spur knuckles.

Lust to bust teeth in the skull.
As when the psalm goads God.

Once: mouse probed verbena.
Hunched, fixed upon crumbs.

Now: pink petals, orange petals.
Xia dynasty Queen peony.

King peony, unclassed until *Qin*.
Full, unforsworn, failing action.

Millennial

11th-century Alamūt assassins.
Or—a shōgun burned temples.

Monk Kaisen just sat—one way.
Calm, blasé to flame.

Recall Vietnamese Buddhists.
I programmed a mainframe.

(Deferred for "critical skills.")
A CO there did alternate service.

What did I know of war?
A brother-in-law's M-16.

Words like *the fires of Dresden*.
(Put, struck, swapped.)

Car bombs leave me whole.
What eye for what eye?

Debris of the universal Kaddish.
Blaspheming local death.

NEW YEAR

Must one be Christ martyr?
I gave the subway guitar man a dollar.

I gave what?
This is America; we have things on our minds.

He picked, piped, looked like a Mayan.
Proud? Irate? Sly?

I wanted what? Love? Salvation? Thanks?
A second came.

Tourists coughed up.
He dissed: "long faces," "600-dollar shoes/jackets."

I was backtracking from a feast.
The gelid air was crystal.

I forget what? Please!
Do dogs parse par?

One is what one arrogates.
Incorrigible, leveraged absolution of witness.

THE TRAIN EXPLODES

The train explodes.
One pays the fare.
Snow falls in a song.
A door closes.

One pays the fare.
There is a platform.
A door closes.
Words explain.

There is a platform.
There is a timetable.
Words explain.
Fate is a metronome.

There is a timetable.
Stars implode.
Fate is a metronome.
Fear halts desire.

Stars implode.
Snow falls in a song.
Fear halts desire.
The train explodes.

LIKE ANYONE

Grace, action, redemption.
Lies, jokes, truth, faking truth.

Teeth gnashed, nauseous, nauseated.

Remembering, forgetting war.
Moments, a day.

Did the back hurt?
Did it hurt to stand?

Hand held by hands.

Anyone, a neighbor, say.
Sick unto death.

Saying what is said of the strength to go on.

Whether or not: strength.
Whether or not: one went on.

Like anyone.

Conquest of Peru

tears wept by the sun

When I am dead: Viracocha yet forges Apu Punchau—solar metal.
Gold noon, emerald-encrusted speculum blinding the dolorous Inca.

When I am dead: Christ's robots yet melt down Qoricancha—gold corral.
Gold floor, 700 gold layers plating granite walls.

When I am dead: Pizarro yet garrotes Atahualpa for Cuzco—world navel.
Gold husks, hymenal royal sun brides nurturing gold cobs.

When I am dead: gold yet exceeds blood.

Without Irony

The songs come up in the coffee bar.
Late in life the visceral amplification of the dyad of power and evil.

So much to arbitrate—without irony.

The century awaits to confer its catastrophe-of-the-century award.
Congruent, perhaps, with plague or the dinosaurs.

The death camps or Hiroshima.
(Man-made of a different moral order.)

I hesitate to mention, without irony, the end of man.
Fixed on his profoundly held notions of right or wrong.

Subverter of charity, for example, in the name of the martyr of charity.

Hammered—like Spartacus on the Starz channel.
(Slave of the arena—starved or fed.)

Hundreds of red palm prints at Chauvet.
One imprinted red negative hand via spat-out red ochre.

Impress of the witness—30, 000 years ago.
(My hand on the glass plate of the scanner.)

No tears, no yes or no, none to mourn the Neanderthal.

Paradisiacal Park Far from War

Tree-blocked light, small blue verbena flowers.
Banana plant's broad, ribbed, yellowish leaves.

Old woman in black on a bench, with pearls and red beret.
But where was her slumped husband sketching in black beret?

Shopping cart like the metal wheeler given a neighbor.
(Fallen in the street, afraid to go out.)

Labor-Day-weekend-Sunday paradisiacal park far from war.
(Absent Twin-Tower abutters of obdurate, cloudless blue.)

•

Saw her again today—red cockade, black beret.
End-of-lifer at stubborn wind, footprinted snow, umbrellaed rain.

As many stride the sidewalk past this natural fraction.
Edging the environing iron of its habitués.

Near the sky-high-rent, world-wide-tourist center of the universe.
(Pre-fashionista, meat-packers' blood-acrid pavements.)

Outpoured, exuberant paradisiacal park far from war.
Burgeoned, last-of-April tulips—red, white, yellow, orange.

"WRITING AND CATASTROPHE"

A witness, a human being from the unharmed world.
—FOR CAROLIN EMCKE

Albania, Kosovo/Kosova, Lebanon, Nicaragua, Pakistan

No poem post "holocaust"
Irony shuts up

Body unable to speak on atrocious Earth

No poem sparks the gap—universe-narrow, atom-wide—
Between act and word

Some lover enacts no difference
Eyes bleeding, palms budding stigmata

•

Masculine, thick, black, straight hair
Black-bra sliver at clipped-on microphone

Inevitable splayed legs

Obscene to contrive her
Obscene to rouse "holocaust"

Traumatized ethnic orphan mouthing syntactic gibberish

Nothing needing paraphrase
Nothing needing to be learned

•

Poem implodes—cannot hold "holocaust"
Sky contracts to a speck

At this level of gravity memory ignites
The victim exhumes himself

Reaffirms his crimes

To exist is to be guilty
This is the black hole of morality

Radio alarm buzzer wakes the justice by the torturers

•

Veneration of her as at parents' graves

Marla Ruzicka

—12/31/1976–4/16/2005

Founder: Campaign for Innocent Victims in Conflict (CIVIC)

spread the word
it will be what we make it

sparks ratchet from the tinder
crackle from the racket of fire and light and are gone

tireless, fearless
against generals, bureaucrats, politicians

her skull touching skull
hem of her black *abaya* clenched in her fist

set on the shoulder of the unveiled woman in *hijab*
who buttresses the dark-eyed, moon-eyed child

corpuscles hiss from the splutter
flare from the pyre drafts

motes rocket, incandesce, and are lost
flecks tick from the holocausts

ingénue *face-splitting* smile
Buddha-girl California smile

petite with curly blonde tresses
pretty, peppy, fiery, vivacious

nicknamed *Bubbles* in Kabul
immolated by a *God car* on the Baghdad airport road

45

her last outcry: "I'm alive"

●

no invader grieved at any funeral or house
no envoy offered help or remorse

from mutilated torso to torso
blogs mocking her even as martyr

Rock Creek Park Rollerblade Queen, Cluster Bomb Girl
spitfire, hurricane, love bomb

manic, anorexic, insomnial
fortified by parties and red wine

avatar of the tendered nipples of Ishtar
registrar of the mutes of the underworld

gladiator of the courage of the vulnerable
novice of no past at the boundary of history

saint of the collateral orphans
paladin weeping for a metal planet

nova emptying its burden of souls
stranger arousing the genital wind

auric-haired *bride Marla*
wrapped in the black *abaya*

like the dawn blistering past blood beyond the background

Unfinished Poem
—for Fran Antman

The Andeans sledge for Morococha copper.

They hoped quick years:
to buy land—or a son from the pit.

In the Cemetery of Heaven,
Rosa Escobar's black mantilla hoods stone.

Two days from Huancavelica.

Magnified, reborn Christ wounds.
Brother: pneumonia corpse at Morococha.

●

I confess that I confess.
I have bought and sold copper, nickel, silver and gold.

One of the sleepers, betting for time.

Dreaming farther and farther into the *barriada*,
past mud and flames.

Like any animal lacing shoes.

Trying to inform the saviors of the people—
we know, we know.

●

History's inherent mercury; extracted silver.
Peru's poorest zone.

Víctor Taype, union head, tortured by the *Commando*.

Antonio Cajachagua, mine leader,
assassinated by *Sendero Luminoso*.

Silicosis, arsenic dust.

Acidic Yauli toxic with metals.
Copper, zinc, iron, manganese, cadmium.

●

Stroller thrust on the blue-dusk Hudson,
to shield a child from the squalor.

Agog at the billionaire condos.
Clerestory water wall, infinity-edge pool.

Crucified by the sun spears.

Scorified sky of fire and dark.
Alloys binding *wrists and neck.*

Silhouetted kayak stroking to Rosa Escobar's brother.

4

POEMS

And the dream poem, which all poems envy and connive to become.
And the naked poem, lacking underwear, thrusting hard abs.
And the great poem, stitched from husks, from high-pitched wings.
And the pure poem—the diamond lyric—that is, the absent text.
And the project poem, booting its laptop, blogging out its heart.
And the prize poem, fleshy with ego, stinking of zoos and sex.
And the prayer poem, hooked addict, still stuttering *God*.
And the avant poem, bloody samurai, never again so red.
And the failed poem, like many, cursing Mother and Father.
And the love poem, loading its bullet lipstick, detonating its Buddha.
And the famed poem, smug as hope, outpacing skulls.
And the conceptual poem—ideal purge—Mutt's soiled urinal.
And the forgotten poem, set free at last, guffawing at its luck.
Is that all?—but for the rasping, breathless, newborn caterwaul?
And the anonymous poem, signed under torture, blinded like Justice.

Art

Father knew . . . Black Hawk had had a wonderful dream.
—Edith M. Teall, 1932

The series started as a dream . . . This idea was not carried out.
—Dorothy M. Caton, 1963

1881 blizzard starves Black Hawk.
Pride cannot feed child or "squaw."

Trader William Caton gives pencils, ink, paper.
Half-dollar credit per chimera.

Black Hawk: *destroyer, buffalo eagle rider.*
Lightning reins, rainbow tail, horned heads, hand/foot/hoof claws.

Draws the Lakota to account the Lakota.
Hunting, courtship, birds, clothes, animals, war.

Linen-backed, leather-bound—willed to heirs via law.
Lost/found in a Goodwill file drawer.

Asset of Dorothy's legatee Bessie Irwin.
Roommate at Rogue Valley Manor.

Auction: 76 plates, 387K, 1994.
Resold to "custodians" Eugene & Clare Thaw.

Envaulted at Cooperstown's Fenimore.
Thwarted thunder guardian, monetized awe.

Murderous Wounded Knee Creek dawn.
She Bear (wife), Weasel Bear (daughter), Black Hawk.

•

If I don't work—who knows?
I am no other; no other is me.

I must practice at this moment.
No other can act—here, now.

STATEMENTS FOR POETRY

1

Not magic, logos, light.
What "hope"?

"Mother of the stupid."
Old joke. Dad's land.

Ergo: Jew. No Pole.
Reason to quote Herbert?

No. Apollo to flay rivals.
Ah!

Such honesty/sincerity.
Such dull/last/only hope.

2

"Honey for flies, not shit."
Who said that?

Doubtless—*Wunderkind.*
But bards fawn.

Exalt the disembarked.
Grin; get signed books.

Epigraph exemplars.
Anthology epitomes.

Homeland Homer hungers.
Wunderkind gorges.

3

At last, past rebate.
Doesn't hate nth rate.

Why not? It's late!
Never or now to inflate.

Puffs up the chest.
Uploads like the rest.

Failed fate/art?
Still—bloody heart!

Up/down, sky/ground.
For love, upside down.

4

Never begged a dollar.
Sun: not lauder or judge.

No bullet cracked ears.
"Worst part of war."

Had women, wed a wife.
One perfume was clear.

Wrote past Millennium.
Not a bad grind.

History: stubborn, shrill.
Mad dreams, dream will.

A GREAT WIND IS BEARING ME ACROSS THE SKY

Dead neighbor's canvases—scrapped.
(The Whitney trashed Jo Hopper.)

Recluse Beauchamp, once hot.
Clued me to archetypes.

Longhand dreams, watercolor mandalas.
Elbe black spring binder (1966).

Mother: temple columns over water.
Devil: horns, stuck-out tongue, hard-on.

Notley's notebooks at UCSD.
Rangy, skeletal, Needles, Barnard girl.

Hit on her on Broadway.
Before she was "Notley."

Seen later with Koch's St. Marks claque.
But don't junk a dream book.

Didn't Sis almost torch Emily?
(Emily, Emily; Hugh, Hugh.)

Who loves poetry? (What else new?)
Do what? Obsess fortune?

Profess physics? Dig ditches?
Sonnet sequences? Saussure's vectors?

Can't afford to check ego at the door?
Not yet hipped to shut up?

O busted art heart!
O heartless Hugh!

Mother dream: a propellered machine.
A colleague strokes my body.

Devilish paradox.
Not, never, "Notley"; never not "Notley."

1928

Mother: Uncle George's steno.
Dollar-a-year man.

Her sister: Aunt Ann.

Father (Monas): night-class "Max."
Liberty Street radio store.

Wed: '34.

Broker, real estate, by then.
Matchmaker: "A.G." Golden?

●

Did Mother shelve the *Rubaiyat*?
Van Doren's *World Poetry*?

"MEMORY OF JOHN DRYDEN"

Brother Carl's first book.
Editor: Lit Guild of America.

Feb. '29.

Pre-crash royalties buy four floors.
Townhouse: 3-9-3 Bleecker.

●

Polytechnic Max: 300 Berriman.
Chem engineer—no MD.

Why not? Kike quota?

Post-work, new-world dark.
Par poor: East New York.

Mark: 34.

Parser of what had been men.
Green-bound, oxidized, thin lignin.

•

WCW, LZ first correspond.
Mark's ex-Columbia kid.

Yiddish: primal tongue.

Bach's *Passion* starts *"A."*
Exile Ez Po prints " 'The.' "

Zuk: 24.

Reads at Les Deux Megots: '61.
Exhorts Max: Don't let poet be son.

L.Z.

tactic of survival
tactic also of competition
—GEORGE OPPEN

Congruent nature/poetic object.
Mathematic of tradition (not by the pants' seat).

Seminal measures inflecting the young.
Rabbinic humility of the radical.

The marathon grinds whomever down.
(Patrons paid Martial millions.)

Fame strives a lifetime to indwell.
Irony of obscurity in real time.

Failure has nothing to be lost.
If bile offend, shall love deform?

Happiness/unhappiness—the great tautology.
Lineage master of the song.

So-called cup of bitterness.
Three times full and running over.

ZUK TAPE

—LOUIS ZUKOFSKY (1904-1978)

Bill Z's note: *Hughie here's Louis*
Craving solace of his voice (decades unheard)

Day past the lashing New Year's Day rain (2003)
(Tape time: " 'A'-20" done, 4 to come)

Lines in my head all my adult life
Blown-dust texts pulled from shelves

Shorter Poems
("Hear her clear mirror"
"Come shadow come")

Bottom
"A"
Catullus
("Miserable Catullus" to "Miss her, Catullus?"
Paradigm of his speech/song poetics)

Barely and Widely

Almost "nerdy" (as one might today say)
Characteristic world-weary sighs

He was born very young in a world that was already very old

As far as dying is concerned
Nobody ever lives through that, said a philosopher

I did my work
I was married
I had a son

As if his riff is the most natural thing in the world
As if any would be as interested as he is in it

Objectivist?
That was forced on me
I had no program
It was all very simple

You live in a world
I don't see how you can escape it
Even if you escape it
You're still living in some kind of situation

You make things in it
You make it with the tools of your own particular craft
In this case words
I feel them as very tangible

Solid so to speak
Sometimes they liquefy
Sometimes they airefy
But those are still existent things

(And finally after over 40 years
I catch "little wrists'" sexual "do")

The brain errs the eye sees
(As per revered Shakespeare)

The form is in that sense organic
All of one's life and this is the life
And for the rest
Nobody else's business

(Discontent? lament?)

It's written in one's time and place
It refers to other times and places as one grows
Whatever way one grows
Takes in

Hopes to survive
Say, well, like Bach's music
It can go down it can go up
That's the interest of it

And all to come through the form of the thing
To hold it together
I don't know
The reader will have to judge

100-year-old World Wide Web face
(Would fame have amazed him?)

"Obscure" man/poet I loved
Total penultimate mesh of words ad infinitum pre-silence

VIENNA

necropoleis of Memphis-*am*-Nile
fortresses of the *Idgasse*
always I have sought the hundred-foot wings of Horus occulting the eyes
         of the goddess
I have outlived Thomas Bernhard in the Café Sacher
though often it seemed I suffered a debilitation that halted me from
         acceding to things as they are
nichts new *meine Herren*
Freud strove on a non-descript block in a waning capitol of a faded
         empire
thus I know how Oedipus triumphed over envy and failure
irony that knows no restraint and that cannot be contained
my head fills with the nouns and verbs of a present imparted by the
         various Attilas from Bosch's Hell
by the waters of the Danube I lay down and slept
drank my dark-chocolate milk as Mother had admonished
this is the best I can do
this is the best I can do
but of course in the Café Sacher I have outlived Thomas Bernhard
         which is no small thing
though in the future an Israeli song mourns on an airport speaker
projecting the millennia of wanderings on the *grosse* Sahara at
         Memphis-*am*-Nile
so that I mull once more why Einstein deserted the poem in
         nineteen-five
I refer to his heretofore secret internment in the loony bin
the photonic drifting of Barbara Richmond's brown hair in its advection
         across the retina
the flash of ego transcending tears that annihilates all connection to the
         good

though I admit it is hard to right wrong
a frailty of nerve
the pretension of being an artist
the endurance and repetition of the riddle of the bitten breast
Sphinx-like on the sands in the evolution of the fittest that takes no prisoners

EINSTEIN ON THE BEACH

The braless redhead axiomatized the real numbers
Her unmediated breasts pressed at her jersey

I distracted myself amid the tensors of the general theory
The physics professor said he would commend me to John Wheeler at
                    Princeton

Sometimes while my parents slept I pondered all night in my small
                    room off the Narrows
I was not a bad kid but innocent

Abstracted from the violent actual universal world
Though I knew it like anyone cut at the start of the world

Time equaling "t" passed light and mass moved

Big-bang stars in the Hubble telescope
Higgs bosons in the hadron collider

In Paris last week I pilgrimed to the site of the Highlander's barge at the
                    Quai de la Tournelle
Dead hero only if he should lose his head

Good versus evil TV morality play for a boy
Warrior not assassin immortal swordsman redheads shedding at last
                    their clothes

The secret and sentimental life of poems
Desire for the beloved raised to the dream power

Invented as I went since none shall judge me any longer
Sick unto death of the couplet

So many thugs in any century how crush them all?
All passports stamped for the underworld

Somewhere a master stands steps his foot from below his cloak to revolve
         the world
Thus there the dervishes whirl to bar the world from destruction

Two Poems

—Adrienne Rich (1929-2012)

1. In an Ill-Lit Formal Space

black chair back nailed with studs
forearms set on dark, bare wood

conservative grey wool dress
lace flourish at half sleeves

wherein at left elbow skulls glare
(a trick of the brain)

your stare almost mocks us
your stare is the four-year-old

locked in the *closet*
*beat*ing *the wall with* her *body*

second photo: Berryman, you, Mary Jarrell
(a suicide, two suicide widows)

female prodigy fronting the phalanx:
seven dark suits—Kunitz to Penn Warren

privilege to expunge yourself
freedom to renounce the dead

2. THE HOPE OF POETRY

Times's front-page obit
snuffed intellect's 83 orbits

paralyzing fear at the head of the subway stairs
chrysalis from which you sprang

autoimmune sun consuming you
arthritic body of the body politic

art calibrated to such fact
engine of measurement

before hospice you had refused meds
to work, to keep lucid

fortitude of who you were
each student's irreducible debt of gratitude

I type this as time stops
I attain the workshop

I graduate to the hopeless cosmos
I labor because of you with the hope of poetry

THE LONGING OF THE NEW WORLD
FOR THE OLD WORLD

I keep my post for you at the harbor of the new world.

I go down at dusk and watch the sun drop.
I see each window luminate in the far-shore monoliths.

I keep my post for you: Liberty statue, benches, boats.

My father landed a hundred years ago from the old world.
Take care, come home, as they say, safe and sound.

I keep my post for you at the bend in the continent.

At the soccer fields, the trapeze school, the tennis courts.
I keep my post for you, toward the Battery, with each step on the
   esplanade.

I gave you the apple to eat on the train to Linz.

When I eat an apple I will think of that bitten apple.
When I drink my coffee I will think of the coffee we drank in the Café
   Prückel.

I will think of you not being beside me on the plane back to the new
   world.

Have a good time at your art school.
I love you; my body is breached by love.

I will pass each hour, work and sleep, keep myself for myself and your
   return.

I will think of you in the old world as I stand in the new world.
This poem conjoins to the absence of Mother.

This poem creates itself as the absence of Mother.

No reason for the poem but the absence of Mother.
No refuge from the absence of Mother but the poem.

I breathe the dark of the water that covers the last of the sky.

For what do the people of the old world long?
Why do they show the American film in the park below the Ferris wheel
                    in the Prater?

I keep my post for you, my river post.

"Nothing amends death but elegy. The road on the front cover is called *Converging Road I*, as if there were others (and there are). A page, perhaps, from a text on perspective or the symbol of a life that narrows to its final point. And the almost-full, smudged moon has arisen once and for all over the inescapable mountains of illumination beyond the dark trees."

—H.S.

Hugh Seidman has published seven poetry books, including *Somebody Stand Up and Sing,* which won the Green Rose Prize from New Issues Press; *Collecting Evidence,* which won the Yale Series of Younger Poets prize; and *People Live, They Have Lives,* which was judged the winner of the Camden Poetry Award. He has also won three New York State poetry grants; three NEA fellowships; and his *Selected Poems: 1965-1995* was named one of the *Village Voice's* "25 Favorite Books of 1995." Seidman has taught at the University of Wisconsin, Yale University, the City College of CUNY, the College of William and Mary, the New School University, and other institutions.

Made in United States
North Haven, CT
04 December 2021

11965466R00052